and *Wirral*

Compiled by
Terry Marsh

publishing

Mapping sourced from Ordnance Survey

Text: Terry Marsh
Photography: Terry Marsh
Editor: Geoffrey Sutton
Designer: Doug Whitworth

© Jarrold Publishing 2002

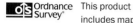
Jarrold Publishing ISBN 0-7117-2026-6

While every care has been taken to ensure the accuracy of the route directions, the publishers cannot accept responsibility for errors or omissions, or for changes in details given. The countryside is not static: hedges and fences can be removed, field boundaries can alter, footpaths can be rerouted and changes in ownership can result in the closure or diversion of some concessionary paths. Also, paths that are easy and pleasant for walking in fine conditions may become slippery, muddy and difficult in wet weather, while stepping-stones across rivers and streams may become impassable.

If you find an inaccuracy in either the text or maps, please write or e-mail to Jarrold Publishing at the addresses below.

First published 2002
by Jarrold Publishing

Printed in Belgium
by Proost NV, Turnhout. 1/02

Jarrold Publishing
Pathfinder Guides, Whitefriars,
Norwich NR3 1TR
E-mail: pathfinder@jarrold.com
www.jarroldpublishing.co.uk/
pathfinders

Front cover: The River Alt at Hightown
Previous page: The Old Mill at Willaston

Contents

ORMSKIRK
WIGAN
West
kayne
Scarth
Hill
Aughton
Park
ORRELL
Up Holland
INCE-IN-
MAKER
M58
Aughton
Higher
End
Bickerstaffe
Crawford
A59
BILLINGE
MAGHULL
Tower Hill
Bryn
Gates
M58
Melling
Crank
Moss
Bank
Garswood
Chadwick
Green
ASHTON-IN-
MAKERFIELD
Stubsha
RAINFORD
KIRKBY
Knowsley
Industrial Park
A570
GOLBORNE
Aintree
HAYDOCK
A580
ST-HELENS
Earlestown
M6
Knowsley
Eccleston
A572
M57
3
Knowsley
Hall
Thatto
Heath
NEWTON-LE-
WILLOWS
West
Derby
PRESCOT
Sutton
Leach
Clock
Face
Burtonwood
HUYTON-WITH-
ROBY
Whiston
Rainhill
Dallam
A57
WARRINGTON
LIVERPOOL
Cronton
Great
Sankey
Childwall
Hough
Green
A557
Bold
Heath
A57
Penketh
A562
Woolton
Tarbock
Green
Farnworth
A561
Allerton
A5300
Ditton
A562
Higher
Walton
Grassendale
Hunt's
Cross
Moore
Garston
Halewood
WIDNES
Daresbury
Hatton
Hale
Bank
A558
Eastham
Sands
Speke
Hall
Hale
16
Norton
Speke
RUNCORN
Halton
Preston on the Hill
Liverpool
Airport
Dungeon
Banks
Weston
Preston-
Brook
Dutton
ELLESMERE
PORT
Ince Banks
Sutton
Weaver
A533
Oil
Refinery
Ince
Aston
Whitby
Little
Stanney
Thornton-
le-Moors
Elton
FRODSHAM
15
Acton
Bridge
Helsby
Newton
Stoak
A5117
4
Weaverham
M56
Hapsford
Alvanley
Crowton
Wervin
Backford
Picton
Dunham-
on-the-Hill
Manley
Norley
Hatchmere

Introduction

The routes and information in this book have been devised specifically with families and children in mind. All the walks include points of interest as well as a question to provide an objective.

If you, or your children, have not walked before, choose from the shorter walks for your first outings, though none of the walks is especially demanding. The purpose is not simply to get from A to B, but to enjoy an exploration, which may be just a steady stroll in the countryside.

The walks are graded by length and difficulty, but few landscapes are truly flat, so even short walks may involve some ascent, though around Merseyside and Wirral this is rarely excessive. Details are given under Route Features in the first information box for each route. But the precise nature of the ground underfoot will depend on recent weather conditions. If you do set out on a walk and discover the going is harder

The summit of Helsby Hill

The village of Thornton Hough

than you expected, or the weather has deteriorated, do not be afraid to turn back. The route will always be there another day, when you are fitter or the children are more experienced or the weather is better.

Bear in mind that the countryside also changes. Landmarks may disappear, gates may become stiles, rights of way may be altered. However, with the aid of the book and its maps you should be able to enjoy many interesting family walks in the countryside.

Merseyside and Wirral

First impressions would not lead one to suppose that Merseyside has much to offer walkers, but that simply isn't true. The heart of the city is unquestionably built up, but even here there are numerous green lungs of country and urban parks and routes that run alongside one of Britain's greatest rivers. Some of these are included in this book, others are left for you to discover for yourself.

North of Liverpool, the Sefton Coast awaits exploration. Here a unique habitat is found, one of the largest sand-dune systems in Britain, extending for miles from Birkdale, near Southport, to the mouth of the Mersey. The sandy hills and hollows are home to hundreds of birds, wild flowers, insects and animals, including some rare or restricted species like the natterjack toad and the red squirrel.

Wirral is a huge peninsula of land bounded by the rivers Mersey and Dee and the Irish Sea. There was a time when it all belonged to the county of Cheshire, but today the northern section is part of the Merseyside metropolitan conurbation.

Wirral's proximity to the industry and commerce of Liverpool and Birkenhead and the influences of North Wales, give the region a fascinating cultural identity and a history as keen as any in Britain. Here are hidden villages, glorious buildings, long-lost seaports where ships bound for Ireland once moored, lighthouses and windmills. Many of the walks that feature in this book make use, in varying degrees, of the course of the Hooton to West Kirby railway line, which has been turned into a magnificent linear country park.

Traditionally, Wirral has been a dormitory for Liverpool workers, or somewhere to spend a sunny weekend. But Wirral has its own identity, something that lies 'over the water' from Liverpool, and a history that

Fields near Willaston

dates back at least to the times of King Alfred, when it was established (probably) as the Hundred of Wirral, though the precise components of a 'hundred' seem to be lost in antiquity.

The greatest influence in opening up Wirral was the arrival of the Roman forces, who had one of their most important strong-holds at Chester. But

Hadlow Station, Willaston

before the Romans, Wirral had been inhabited by man from Neolithic times and by dinosaurs from an even earlier period. When the Romans reached this part of Britain, Wirral was occupied by the Cornovii, a Celtic tribe who came into Cheshire from Shropshire, and Celtic influences still remain, particularly in some of the place-names.

In Roman times the shape of Wirral and the coastlines of the two rivers would have been significantly different, with much of the original coast-line now far inland, and great swathes of the estuary reclaimed. With Chester as the great attraction, the Dee Estuary, now a delightful haven for wildfowl, would have been a busy thoroughfare for shipping.

Reaching a little further afield, but still in sight of the River Mersey, the book takes the opportunity to explore the area around Frodsham and Helsby, two enormous sandstone escarpments with a view across the unglamorous, industrial side of the Mersey, but with much local interest by way of compensation.

● Woodland wildlife ● interesting hedgerows ● waterfall ● lake

1 *Arrowe Country Park*

Arrowe Country Park is immensely
popular with the local people, and this
walk makes the most of it, wandering
through it and out across adjacent farmland before returning. A patient visitor,
one prepared to wait for a while, may be
treated to the darting flight of a kingfisher
near the lake.

START Arrowe Hill
DISTANCE 2½ miles (4km)
TIME 1 hour
PARKING Arrowe Brook
Road (car park, free)
ROUTE FEATURES Woodland
paths, farm tracks and
fields

Arrowe Country Park is the
largest park in Wirral, compris-
ing 400 acres (162 ha). Nearly two-
thirds are devoted to open parkland
and deciduous woodland containing
many fine examples of oak, ash,
beech, Scots pine and cedar. There
are also some less well-known
species, including redwood, cedar of
Lebanon, maidenhair and Indian
Bean trees. Here are numerous
familiar woodland birds – magpies,
jays, nuthatches, treecreepers and
woodpeckers.

Go to the far end of the car
park, and leave along a broad track
leading into woodland. This is
soon joined by a second track, and
at the junction bear left alongside a
stream on the right.

After about ¼ mile (400m), the
track forks. Branch right Ⓐ along
a path signposted to the 'Lake and
Waterfall'.

Almost immediately, turn right on
to a narrow path that soon crosses
a wooden footbridge, and keep
forward to a step-stile at the
woodland edge, giving into an
large field.

Turn left and follow the field
boundary to a corner, and there

PUBLIC TRANSPORT Bus services along Arrowe Brook Road
REFRESHMENTS None on route
PUBLIC TOILETS None on route
ORDNANCE SURVEY MAPS Explorer 266 (Wirral & Chester), Landranger 108
(Liverpool)

cross a step-stile into the next field. Turn right and walk along the field margin until it meets the end of a farm lane at a metal gate. Ignore this, and keep forward over another stile, then walking with a fence on the left to meet a road.

B At the road, turn left, and follow it for ¼ mile (400m), taking care against approaching traffic. Just before the first house on the left, turn left on to a broad track flanked by hedgerows and wild flowers.

After about 600 yds (550m), immediately on crossing a sleeper bridge, leave the main track and turn left into the adjoining field.

A farm lane, Arrowe Country Park

> **?** Among the trees in the park and the field hedgerows, there are examples of the only British tree to have black buds. What is the name of this tree?

C Continue along the left-hand field margin, alongside a well-established hedgerow, with a wide range of trees. This is especially popular in season with a wide range of butterflies, including speckled wood, small heath and meadow brown.

Cross an intermediate track and go into the next field, keeping forward along the left-hand edge of the field.

At the far side of the field, return to the woodland of Arrowe Country Park, by passing through a hedge gap on to a brief, undulating path that leads to the main woodland track a short distance ahead.

At the main track, beside a low waterfall, turn left. Follow the main track, and soon pass an elongated lake.

Beyond the end of the lake, keep going forward across a bridge, and soon rejoin the outward route. A short way on, keep left along the main track and follow this to return to the car park, remembering to bear right when the track next forks. ●

Crossing open ground

Burton Wood

START Burton
DISTANCE 1½ miles (2.4km)
TIME 1 hour
PARKING Limited on-street parking (park with consideration)
ROUTE FEATURES Mainly woodland paths

2

This is a brief excursion into the lovely mixed woodland of Burton Wood, sometimes called Burton Mill Wood. Burton is a lovely village, and the wood a cool, green oasis on a hot day.

Begin from the centre of Burton village, near the telephone box. Cross the road and go up a slanting track (the Rake), that passes in front of a thatched cottage.

Burton is an attractive village of mixed cottages and houses, many thatched, many of red sandstone, many actually built on the sandstone bedrock, as if the village had simply grown from the earth.

There was a time when Burton was important to Wirral's economy, serving as a port for the crossing to Ireland, until the silting-up of the Dee Estuary and the improvement of roads through North Wales made Holyhead a better and safer option.

Follow the rising track between cottages and up towards Burton Wood (which is also known as Burton Mill Wood), where, at Rake Cottage, a flight of sandstone steps leads you up into the woodland.

Nearby **Burton Manor**, now a college, is a large Edwardian house built for a son of Prime Minister Gladstone, the most appealing feature of which is a small inner courtyard. Over the entrance of the house is the Gladstone coat of arms, which contains a reminder that some of the family wealth was based on the slave trade.

PUBLIC TRANSPORT Bus services to Burton
REFRESHMENTS Nothing in village. Ness or Ness Gardens
PUBLIC TOILETS None on route
ORDNANCE SURVEY MAPS Explorer 266 (Wirral & Chester), Landranger 117 (Chester & Wrexham)

> **Along the way an old windmill is passed. What date was it built?**

A In the woodland, turn left to follow a signposted path along the woodland boundary with cottage gardens on the left. Keep to the boundary path as much as possible, and eventually this leads out to meet a lane at another sandstone step-stile and kissing-gate.

Turn right, up the lane as far as the entrance to a large house called Millwood, where an enclosed path leads back into the woodland.

A few strides along this path reach the circular remains on an old windmill **B**, beyond which the path re-enters the main body of Burton Wood.

Bear left on an obvious path, and then keep forward, always following the main path, ignoring side paths (though overgrowth can make this a little confusing at some times of year). The general direction, however, is always forward.

Eventually the path intercepts another at a T-junction **C**, not far from a wood carving concealed in the undergrowth – a crocodile, perhaps, or a praying mantis?

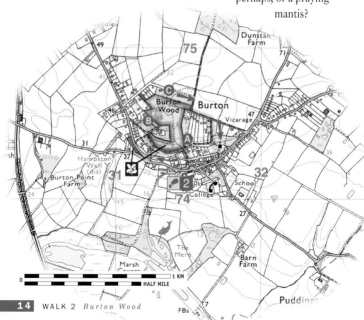

A picturesque thatched cottage at Burton

Turn right at the junction, soon after which the path reaches a picnic area. On entering this, bear half-right to locate another path leaving the area, and heading out to meet a broad track at a wooden barrier.

Turn right and follow the track to a lane (at another barrier), on the edge of the woodland.

Go left, now with detached houses and bungalows on the right. Follow this track for about 150 yds (137m) to a signposted footpath on the right.

> **St Nicholas' Church** is 18th century, though it contrives to have an early 14th-century east window.

Turn right through a metal kissing-gate, on to the path, which leads back into Burton Wood. At a path junction ahead, turn left and go down a sandstone-stepped path to enter the churchyard of St Nicholas' Church.

Keep forward through the churchyard to the gate, and there turn right along a stony lane, almost immediately going left to walk down to meet the main road through the village of Burton, opposite Puddington Lane. From here, turn right to return to the start. ●

3 *Croxteth Country Park*

START Croxteth Country Park main car park
DISTANCE 2 miles (3.2km)
TIME 1 hour
PARKING Through main gates and along drive
ROUTE FEATURES Estate paths

Croxteth Country Park is an outstanding green oasis in the heart of Liverpool. This short walk wanders around its edge, but there is much for children to do here, including picnics, seeing farm animals, visiting the hall and walled garden, and making good use of the adventure play areas.

The 500-acre (200-ha) **Croxteth Hall Country Park** is at the heart of what was once a huge estate stretching hundreds of square miles, the ancestral home of the Molyneux family, the earls of Sefton. It is now one of the Nort West's major heritage centres and has three main attractions (admission charges apply, though the grounds are free): the hall, Home Farm and the Victorian Walled Garden.

Begin from the main car park, and leave at its far end on to a broad estate road soon dipping through an arch that carries Croxteth Hall Lane. Beyond, the road leads up to Croxteth Hall.

On reaching the hall, turn right (Home Farm and an adventure play area are off to the right) and walk as far as the entrance to the café. Bear left, still on a broad estate road. At the rear of the hall, bear right on a road that is signposted to Cocked Hat Wood and Stand Farm.

The track leads on through gates Ⓐ. Go forward into Knowsley Drive. After this crosses a stone footbridge spanning a stream, branch left when the continuing gravel track forks.

PUBLIC TRANSPORT Bus services to main gates
REFRESHMENTS Café in grounds and refreshment vans
PUBLIC TOILETS Near car park and in grounds
ORDNANCE SURVEY MAPS Explorer 275 (Liverpool, St Helens, Widnes & Runcorn), Landranger 108 (Liverpool)

Now follow a delightful path along the edge of paddocks and then through light, mixed woodland.

The track eventually runs alongside a modern housing estate and further on swings left away from the estate. It continues through woodland and comes out to meet another surfaced estate road. Keep left along this, soon passing a wooden barn-like building on the right and the former kennels on the left.

Croxteth Hall

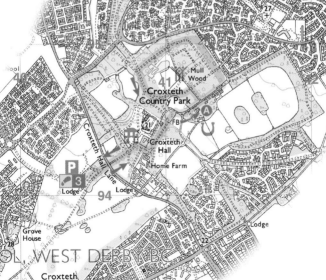

> On the hall gable, a large rectangular fresco features above a white doorway at the top of steps. This depicts military items, weapons, flags and drums. How many 'guns' of any type can you identify?

The road leads back into the central area of the country park. When it forks, bear left (signposted Hall, Farm and Gardens). The road leads back to the junction with Knowsley Drive Ⓐ. Here, turn right through gates to head back towards the hall.

Walk around the back of the hall and then right, along its gable end to reach the front of the hall.

On drawing level with the front of the hall, turn left to go back along the road to the car park. ●

The lily pond at Croxteth Country Park

Helsby Hill

START Helsby
DISTANCE 1½ miles (2.4km)
TIME 1 hour
PARKING Helsby Quarry car park, Alvanley Road
ROUTE FEATURES Woodland paths, unprotected cliff edges, modest ascent

This short walk is a delight and combines pleasant woodland walking with some fine viewpoints. It is especially agreeable in spring and early summer when the trees are alive with birdsong. Note that the path and summit have unprotected cliff edges, so children should be kept under close control.

The walk begins from the Helsby Quarry car park on Alvanley Road. Leave the car park at its far end, turn left on to the road and almost immediately go right into Hill Road South (signposted to Helsby Hill).

Climb steadily to a gate, beyond which the road surfacing ends, and a path goes forward into Helsby Hill (a National Trust property).

> ? At which high point on this walk can you find 'BM S 3499'?

Heading for Helsby Hill

PUBLIC TRANSPORT Bus services to Helsby
REFRESHMENTS None on route
PUBLIC TOILETS None on route
ORDNANCE SURVEY MAPS Explorer 267 (Northwich & Delamere Forest, Winsford), Landranger 108 (Liverpool)

Keep ahead on a gently ascending path through woodland.

When the track forks, bear right along a rising path below a low sandstone cliff wall 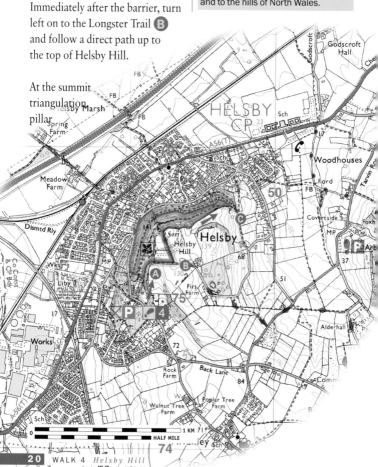. The path later continues between hedgerows to a wooden barrier.

Immediately after the barrier, turn left on to the Longster Trail **B** and follow a direct path up to the top of Helsby Hill.

At the summit triangulation pillar

The view of Helsby from Helsby Hill

turn right to locate a narrow path descending into woodland along the escarpment.

Beyond the cliff edges the path descends agreeably through mixed woodland, finally going down steps to meet a broad track **C**, left and right.

Turn left. The path leads back on to National Trust land and becomes a pleasant terrace walk through woodland.

Keep forward, always following the main path and ignoring branching paths until finally the path runs out to meet a road.

At the road, turn left, taking care against approaching traffic, and follow the road back to the Helsby Quarry car park. ●

5 *Storeton Wood*

START Storeton
DISTANCE 3 miles (4.8km)
TIME 1½ hours
PARKING Layby in side road at Storeton
ROUTE FEATURES Woodland paths, farm tracks and fields

There is no obvious sign today that Storeton Wood was once an important quarry, one that has been in use for 2,000 years. A Roman soldier is said to haunt the wood, and he may have more information, but this peaceful tract of countryside is today a tranquil place to walk and a roost for bats.

From the side-road in Storeton, walk north and follow Little Storeton Lane round to the top end of the village. Turn right and walk down the broad main street.

The main street in Storeton is flanked by rows of sycamore trees, part of a system of **avenues** laid out between 1912 and 1914 for Lord Leverhulme.

Just beyond Lodge Farm Ⓐ, the track ends. Keep going forward on a narrow grassy path between hedgerows, to a dilapidated metal kissing-gate giving into a large field.

Go down to the far end of the road and at a roundabout turn left into Red Hill Road. Bear right with the road and go across the end of Rest Hill Road and, a few strides further on, bear right on to a broad track which passes to the right of a red-brick house.

Go ahead, straight across the field to the far right-hand corner, alongside the M53 motorway. Follow the motorway fence to a stile in a field corner, beyond which an enclosed narrow path continues behind boarding - kennels to meet a lane.

PUBLIC TRANSPORT Bus services to Storeton
REFRESHMENTS None on route
PUBLIC TOILETS None on route
ORDNANCE SURVEY MAPS Explorer 266 (Wirral & Chester), Landranger 108 (Liverpool)

The white sandstone formerly quarried in Storeton Wood has been used in many buildings. But one especially is world-renowned: tall and American. What is it?

Near Storeton

Turn left. When the road bends left **B**, leave it on the right over a step-stile on to a signposted path for Higher Bebington. Cross fields, aiming for a conspicuous black-and-white footpath signpost in the distance.

On leaving the fields, bear briefly left to a road and turn right

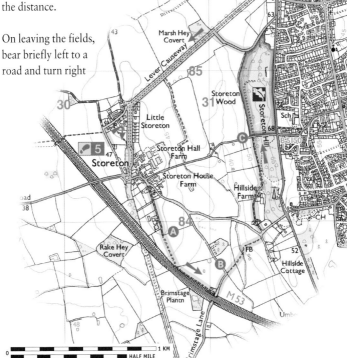

for a few strides, immediately going left on a signposted path to Rest Hill Road. This skirts adjacent property and leads up to a broad vehicle track along the edge of woodland.

Follow the track, which runs out to meet a road. Go forward to enter Storeton Wood **C**, a Woodland Trust property.

One of the avenues of trees on the route

Go forward on the left-hand of two tracks. Soon enter the woodland along the raised trackbed.

The woodland walk finally ends at a gate giving on to a road. Turn left, and follow the road to a T-junction. Here, turn left along another drive (Lever Causeway) flanked by trees.

This drive leads to the northern edge of Storeton. Here turn right into Little Storeton Lane, and then follow the lane round to return to the starting point in the village of Storeton. ●

Brimstage and Thornton Hough

6

START Brimstage
DISTANCE 3 miles (4.8km)
TIME 1½ hours
PARKING At rear of craft centre
ROUTE FEATURES Woodland paths, farm tracks and fields

This delightful tour of the countryside between Brimstage and Thornton Hough largely crosses Leverhulme estate lands and is one of the most appealing walks in this book. There are far-reaching views and two attractive villages to take in – and all the attractions of historical Brimstage.

Start from the car park at the rear of the craft centre in Brimstage by crossing a step-stile and the field

Brimstage Hall boasts a magnificent stone tower, thought to be part of, or pre-date, an oratory that Sir Hugh Hulse was granted a licence to build at Brimstage in 1398. The tower is certainly much older than the hall itself, and some believe it dates from the early 12th century. The whole of the building occupied by the Craft Centre is a Grade I Listed Building of some considerable importance. And the small paddock on the right is believed to be an ancient village site.

beyond to meet up with the A5137. Turn left along the A-road for a little over 100 yds (91m), and then turn left into Talbot Avenue.

Almost immediately go left again at a metal gate to gain access to a footpath (signposted to Thornton Hough). This goes forward as a grassy path flanked by mature hedgerows and is a delightfully shaded walk on a warm day, dappled by sunlight and alive with birdsong.

The continuing path leads to a step-stile (with a yellow waymark),

PUBLIC TRANSPORT Bus services to Brimstage and Thornton Hough
REFRESHMENTS Country Mouse Restaurant at craft centre, pubs in Thornton Hough
PUBLIC TOILETS None on route
ORDNANCE SURVEY MAPS Explorer 266 (Wirral & Chester), Landranger 108 (Liverpool)

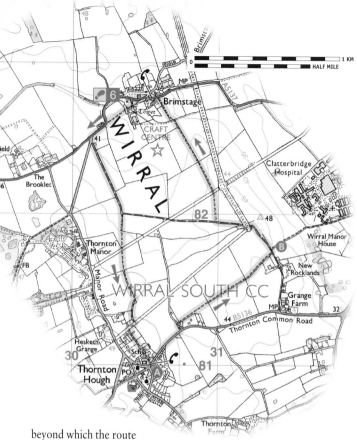

beyond which the route continues along the left-hand field edge, still going forward.

When the hedge-row on the left changes direction, cross another stile and go over the ensuing field to a metal kissing-gate in the far right-hand corner.

Off to the right stands the imposing **Thornton Manor**, once the home of Lord Leverhulme, which he bought in 1891, having rented it since 1888. The manor was originally a modest early-Victorian building that Leverhulme transformed into the present-day neo-Elizabethan mansion.

Through the gate, cross a driveway to another kissing-gate opposite, and then follow a clear path across an arable field, heading for a small stand of Scots pine.

On the far side of the field, go forward alongside

a hawthorn hedgerow on the right to a step-stile in a field corner. Over this, go forward along the edge of the next field to another stile giving on to another enclosed and shaded path through woodland.

> ? *Thornton Manor was the home of Lord Leverhulme, a famous industrialist. One of the things he manufactured was soap. What was the name of the soap, after which he named an estate village?*

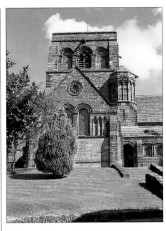

St George's Church, Thornton Hough

This emerges at an estate road. Here, turn right, for about 30 yds (27m), and then go left on to a broad gravel track between hedgerows and soon pass along the edge of a farm, going forward to

> **Thornton Hough** is a beautiful estate village that was the work of two landlords, Joseph Hirst, a textile manufacturer from Yorkshire, and Viscount Leverhulme. The village, which contains many attractive buildings, groups around its two churches: All Saints', a rock-faced red sandstone building, and the dominant St George's, designed for Lord Leverhulme in the Norman style, and reflecting Lord Leverhulme's non-Conformist beliefs. Today it is part of the United Reformed Church, and entered through a charming hexagonal covered entranceway, also Norman in style.

meet the B5136 on the edge of Thornton Hough **A**.

At the B-road turn left and follow the road for about 300 yds (274m) and then, just on reaching the first cottage on the left, leave the road for a signposted path on the left for Clatterbridge.

The path soon changes direction, and, beyond a step-stile, runs along a field edge. When the hedgerow on the right changes direction, keep forward across an arable field to follow a row of overhead powerlines and passing into the next field at a hedge gap.

Continue in the same direction, now with a hedge on the right, but

The gatehouse of Thornton Manor

still following overhead lines. Keep to the path across two fields. On entering the second field, the two cathedrals of Liverpool come into view in the far distance.

At a broad gravel track **B**, turn left and pass a metal gate, continuing along the track as it bends left to a track junction. Ignore the broad tracks left and right, but go forward on to a sign-posted footpath into a small woodland copse to follow a narrow path along the woodland edge.

Continue for about 200 yds (183m) to a signposted path on the right, leaving the woodland at a hedge gap to cross a large open field to a gap on the other side giving on to an estate road.

Cross to a stile opposite, beyond which keep forward along the left-hand field edge. At the far end of the field, go ahead, now with a hedgerow on the right. The field edge path leads to a stile. Over this, cross the end of another field to a stile, giving on to a farm access.

Cross the access and, over another stile, go forward along a sparse hedgerow to reach the road on the edge of Brimstage.

Turn left to return to the craft centre car park at the starting point. ●

West Kirby

START Wirral Country Park, Caldy
DISTANCE 3¾ miles (5.2km)
TIME 2 hours
PARKING Car park at start
ROUTE FEATURES Old track-bed, marine promenade

7

West Kirby is popular at any time of year. The seafront is haunted by hardy locals even in the direst of weather conditions and on a sunny day it is thronged, the beaches packed, the marine lake full to overflowing with yachtsmen and wind-surfers and the whole atmosphere one of seaside fun.

The course of the railway trackbed is understandably easy to follow, and these days is flanked by a wide wide variety of **plantlife** and trees that are host to an even wider variety of **birdlife**. Keep an eye out for bullfinches and long-tailed tits and also the occasional green woodpecker.

Begin from the Wirral Country Park car park at Caldy, leaving at the far end of the car park on to the right-hand of three paths that appear, going forward to link up with the trackbed of the former Hooton to West Kirby railway line.

On the marine lake, West Kirby

PUBLIC TRANSPORT Bus services to Caldy and West Kirby
REFRESHMENTS A whole range of options in West Kirby
PUBLIC TOILETS West Kirby
ORDNANCE SURVEY MAPS Explorer 266 (Wirral & Chester), Landranger 108 (Liverpool)

The sea is kept a little at bay by a large **marine lake**. With the tide in, people walking around the lake look as through they are walking on the water.

West Kirby, strange as it may seem today, was once quite a place of iniquity as a large floating population of travellers, waiting for favourable winds to carry them to Ireland, made full use of the town's many inns. Surprisingly, one of the popular haunts was the rectory, which an over-ambitious curate turned into a public house.

After a little over 1 mile (1.6km), the trackbed suddenly ends at a gate giving on to the A540 **A** on the edge of West Kirby. Through the gate, turn left into Elder Grove and go forward, to follow the main road past shops and as far as Barclays Bank, and there turn left into Dee Lane (signposted West Kirby Marine Lake).

Walk down to the far end of Dee Lane, where it turns left along the seafront **B**.

West Kirby

Jetty
Sailing School

21

Marine Lake

Tanskey Rocks

IRB Sta

86

Tell's Tower

Lime Wharf

87

Grange Hill
War Meml Cem

A540

Wirral Way

Sch

Caldy Hill

Caldy

38

B5140

85

P 7

0   1 KM
HALF MILE

Mean Low Wa

A view of West Kirby from Caldy Hill

A pedestrian promenade runs around the lake, beginning at the end of Dee Lane. Go on to this and follow the walkway (sometimes wet if the tide is in and the wind a little fresh) all the way to South Parade, where it ends. On very blustery days it may be easier to follow the main promenade.

On leaving the marine walk, go forward to a road junction and into Sandy Lane. Keep on up Sandy Lane, climbing gently to cross the

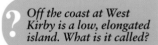

Off the coast at West Kirby is a low, elongated island. What is it called?

old railway line. On the other side of the bridge, turn right into York Avenue and go immediately right, down steps, to rejoin the railway trackbed **C**.

Turn left and follow the trackbed back to the starting point at Caldy car park. ●

● Coastal sand-dunes ● pine woodland ● wildlife ● wild flowers

8 *Formby Hills*

START Victoria Road, Formby
DISTANCE 3½ miles (5.6km)
TIME 2 hours
PARKING National Trust car park at end of Victoria Road
ROUTE FEATURES Roads, woodland paths, tracks, sand-dunes and beach

The road walking is modest and leads to a delightful circuit of wildlife habitats created by sand-dunes. The walk can be extended by including the 'Squirrel Walk' in the Nature Reserve; red squirrels are abundant here, but often difficult to spot. Note that at certain times of year, jellyfish and weaver fish become stranded on the beach or in the shallows. These are capable of stinging anyone who stands on them bare-footed. For this reason, always ensure that children on the beach wear shoes or sandals at all times.

Leave the car park by walking back towards Victoria Road. On

The **nature reserve** is part of the fourth-largest sand-dune system in Britain and includes inter-tidal sand flats and both high yellow dunes and fixed dunes. The sand-dunes at Formby are constantly changing and can move dramatically. Marram grass was planted on the dunes to help stop them moving. At the moment the frontal dunes are being worn away by the sea, and currently lose about 13ft (4m) a year.

the way there is a chance to divert into the woods on the right to follow the Squirrel Walk Ⓐ.

Continue past the entrance to the National Trust land. Keep on along Victoria Road, as far as Freshfield station.

Just after the railway crossing, turn left into Montagu Road (sign-posted: Fisherman's Path 500m), and walk past the station car park.

PUBLIC TRANSPORT Rail and bus services to Freshfield (the walk can start from the station), then NT Beach bus service from station
REFRESHMENTS Formby has numerous pubs and cafés; ice-cream vendors visit the car park
PUBLIC TOILETS Within woodland, adjoining main access
ORDNANCE SURVEY MAPS Explorer 285 (Southport & Chorley, Wigan, Formby), Landranger 108 (Liverpool)

This is one of the best places in England to see the **red squirrel**. Elsewhere they have declined due to disease and competition from grey squirrels, and are now rare or absent altogether. The woods have only been here for around 100 years. They were planted to provide shelter for crops and to limit sand blow.

At the end of the car park there is a choice. Either continue on the surfaced lane, or branch left on to a sandy path that runs alongside the railway line. Both routes rejoin later.

Beyond the end of the road-surfacing lies

Freshfield Dune Heath **B**, an open area of scrubland with a wide range of trees and shrubs. Here bear left on a broad track still beside the railway line. Continue to reach a level-crossing (signposted: Public footpath to beach 1 mile).

Cross the line with care (the trains are quite frequent), and on the

In 1990 there was a severe storm along the Sefton Coast. How many metres of sand-dune were lost during that storm. Check the information panels near the squirrel walk to find out.

Ainsdale
National Nature
Reserve

Cloven-le-Dale

Sefton Coastal Footpath

Fisherman's Path

C

Formby Hills

Dale Slack Gutter

Dunes

Dunes

D

27

28

09

29

Caravan Park

P 8

Dunes

A

V

Freshfield

B

Sch

PC

0   1 KM
HALF MILE

Sandfield Farm

other side join the Fisherman's Path; a broad track developed many years ago when sea fishing was a major part of the local economy.

Immediately the path crosses Formby Golf Course (Beware low-flying golf balls!), but soon enters a wooded area leading to the Ainsdale Sand Dunes National Nature Reserve **C**.

On entering the reserve, keep forward on a broad track to follow a line of white-topped posts. The continuing track wanders through delightful mixed woodland, but eventually runs on into sand-dunes. Keep going forward, with a low fence on the right. When the sandy path forks, bear left along the

Sefton Coastal Footpath **D**.

The way through the dunes continues to be marked by white-topped posts. Suddenly the path breaks free of the dunes and bursts out on to the beach. Turn left along the beach. To the north can be seen Blackpool Tower set against the hazy blue of the Lakeland Fells. To the south, ferries and cargo vessels sail out from Liverpool against the backdrop of the mountains of North Wales.

Warning: At certain times of year, jellyfish and weaver fish become stranded on the beach or in the shallows. These are capable of stinging anyone who stands on them bare-footed. For this reason, always ensure that children on the beach wear shoes or sandals at all times.

Continue along the beach as far as a beacon marked 'Victoria Road South' and here leave the beach by turning left up through the dunes to return to the car park and start. ●

On the Fisherman's Path, Formby

Irby and Thurstaston Common

START Telegraph Road (A540), Thurstaston

DISTANCE 3½ miles (5.6km)

TIME 2 hours

PARKING At start

ROUTE FEATURES Roads, woodland paths, farm tracks and fields

For all its modest height, Thurstaston Hill provides one of the finest panoramas in Wirral, rising only a short distance from the centre of Irby. The nominal ascent of the hill is optional, providing an added bonus to an already delightful circuit.

Start from the Thurstaston Common car park along the A540 (here Telegraph Road). Leave the car park and turn left, walking past the nearby pub to a crossroads. Here turn left into Thurstaston Road.

Thurstaston Common

About 30 yds (27m) into Thurstaston Road, turn right on to a footpath signposted to Irby. Go forward past a building and, on the other side, cross a concrete stile on the left. Keep to the right of the ensuing field, pass a small pond and then cross to a step-stile in the far left-hand corner of the field.

Over the stile, walk along an enclosed path into a small housing estate (Dawlish Rd). Turn right and go on to a signposted path for Irby. This leads to a stile into a field. Bear left along the field edge to a kissing-gate opposite a busy road junction.

PUBLIC TRANSPORT Bus services along A540 and to Irby (alternative start)

REFRESHMENTS Irby has pubs and cafés, and there are pubs on the way

PUBLIC TOILETS None on route

ORDNANCE SURVEY MAPS Explorer 266 (Wirral & Chester), Landranger 108 (Liverpool)

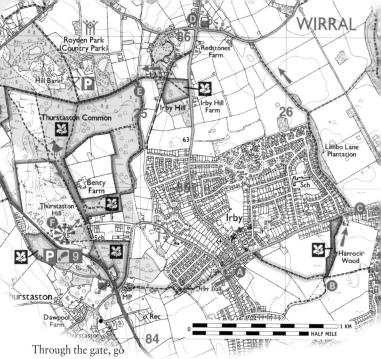

Through the gate, go forward into Thingwall Avenue and walk through the centre of Irby **A**. Just beyond the last shops, turn on to a footpath on the right (signposted Lower Pensby). This soon becomes an enclosed path between fence and hedgerow.

When the path gives into a large field, keep left alongside a hedgerow. Follow this to a wooden gate at the southern edge of Harrock Wood **B**. Cross a small stream and climb to the gate opposite. A few strides further on, turn left through another gate, giving into the woodland.

Follow a narrow woodland path until, eventually, it meets a road. At the road turn right.

Cross the road with care. On the left a parallel road appears, with a mini-roundabout at its end. Immediately after the roundabout, leave the main road by turning left on to a broad woodland path **C** with arable fields on the right.

Continue to the end of the track, at a road, and there turn left. Follow the road with care to a junction near the Irby Mill pub **D**, and here turn left into Mill Hill road.

Cross to the footpath opposite and, on reaching Sandy Lane North, turn right on to a stony track between high gorse hedgerows.

Follow the lane past a row of bungalows and stay with it as it bends right. Go past the entrance to September Cottage and, a short way further on, as the lane bends to the right, leave it, on the apex of the bend, to pass Hazeldene and turn right on to a narrow descending path beside a close-boarded fence.

> **?** *Just by Irby Branch Library there is an item of medieval punishment. What is it?*

The path leads down to the entrance to Thurstaston Common **E**. Go down steps on the left and cross a footbridge, climbing into light woodland on the other side.

The path soon runs alongside a drystone wall. When the wall ends, keep forward in the same direction to meet another wall, at a wall corner. Keep forward alongside this second wall and, when it changes direction abruptly, leave its

Thurstaston Common nature reserve is the finest remaining example of a lowland heathland in the North-West. It supports a range of rare and unusual plants and wild creatures and is especially beautiful when the heather is in bloom in August and September.

company for a track, going left.

Now follow a clear path through the woodland to a gate and continue beyond. Keep on to pass Benty's Farm, and about 100 yds (91m) later, leave the broad track for a narrow path through bracken into woodland on the right.

The path leads to a kissing-gate giving on to a surfaced lane. Move slightly right to the foot of a sandstone path climbing the nearby hillside. This is Thurstaston Hill **F**, which is easily included in the walk.

Retrace the path to the foot of the hill and turn right to resume the original direction. The continuing path eventually leads out to meet the A540 only a short distance away from the car park at the starting point.

The view from **Thurstaston Hill** is extensive, reaching as far as Blackpool on the Fylde Coast, the hills of the West Pennine Moors, the sand-dunes of the Sefton Coast, the cathedrals of Liverpool, and, of course, the Dee Estuary and the coastline of North Wales.

10 *Around Heswall*

START Heswall Shore
DISTANCE 3½ miles (5.6km)
TIME 2 hours
PARKING Banks Road, Heswall
ROUTE FEATURES Woodland paths, tracks and field paths

This modest walk visits one of Wirral's hidden gems, the Dales, a delightful reserve of mixed woodland and heather, especially beautiful in August and September.

Leave the car park and walk back up Banks Road, taking care against approaching traffic. As the road turns right, follow it and shortly go left to cross a railway bridge. Keep forward, climbing gently, and soon turn left into Pipers Lane **A**.

Continue past the end of Crossley Drive and 30 yds (27m) later, leave the road by turning right on to a signposted path for the Dales.

The continuing path climbs between houses into mixed wood-land. Ignore a turning on the left and keep forward to a low yellow waymark, and there bear right, climbing gently to a wooden barrier.

Through the barrier turn left, still ascending gently into the Heswall Dales Local Nature Reserve and shortly, at a path junction, turn sharply left on to a path that undulates pleasantly through light woodland of birch, rowan, gorse, oak and banks of heather, and with lovely views out across the Dee Estuary.

Always keep following the main path, ignoring any branching

PUBLIC TRANSPORT Bus services to Banks Road (Heswall Shore)
REFRESHMENTS None on route
PUBLIC TOILETS At start
ORDNANCE SURVEY MAPS Explorer 266 (Wirral & Chester), Landranger 108 (Liverpool)

paths (of which there are many). Eventually leave the reserve at a wooden barrier.

Turn right on to a broad access track and climb gently to a path junction. Here, bear right, still on a broad access, and go up to meet a lane (Oldfield Road). Turn left and, when the road ends, keep forward on to a gravel track (signposted to Thurstaston) **B**.

Keep following the track as it passes Oldfield Farm and, on

The Wirral Way crosses the boundary of two parishes. What are they? Look for a small parish boundary marker for the answers.

the far side of the farm, turn on to a field access track alongside a sandstone wall. This leads to a sandstone stile. Over this, go on to an enclosed path around the edge of a field.

The path runs on into the end of a wooded ravine, known

The foreshore, Heswall

locally as the Dungeon **C**. At the top edge of the woodland, turn left on to a path signposted to the Wirral Way.

Walk down through the woodland on a constructed path, either of concrete slabs or railway sleepers (slippery when wet) to reach a wooden footbridge spanning a small stream.

Beyond the bridge the stream drops over a waterfall into a moss- and fern-covered ravine, while the path maintains a higher level above the ravine. When the continuing path forks, branch left, descending to a path T-junction at the top of steps. Go

down the steps and at the bottom turn right on to a constructed path running down the field edge to meet the Wirral Way.

Turn left on the Wirral way, a raised, former railway trackbed. After 200 yds (183m) look for a signed path on the right, leading down to Heswall Fields and the Beach, a National Trust property. A wood gate gives access to Heswall Fields **D**, and there bear initially left on a grassy path but gradually moving towards the foreshore.

The path leads to an access in a field corner. Go on to a narrow path through brambles that leads down to the foreshore. Turn left and walk along the foreshore.

Keep going, passing a boatbuilder's yard and Shellie's Beach Bar **E**. Immediately after the pub, turn left up a beach access track leading back into the car park at Banks Road. ●

The **Dee Estuary** is renowned for the large numbers and variety of its birdlife, many of them passing by in spring and autumn, while others spend the winter here. The estuary is also famed for its grey seal colonies.

Storeton and Landican

This is a simple and attractive walk from which the nearby motorway is largely hidden, both in sight and sound. The walk links two small villages and skirts the edge of a third. In summer the hedgerows are loud with birdsong and bright with wild flowers and butterflies.

START Storeton
DISTANCE 3¾ miles (6km)
TIME 2 hours
PARKING Layby in side road at Storeton
ROUTE FEATURES Farm tracks and field paths

11

Begin from a small layby along the road linking the round-about at the edge of Storeton with Little Storeton Lane. Walk north and, as the road bends right, go forward on to a broad track (Landican Lane).

The track is flanked by farm fields and hedgerows rich in flowers and leads down to run briefly alongside

> At the start you pass one of a number of uniquely styled mileposts that form part of the National Cycle Network. How many mileposts are there in all?

The name **Landican** derives from the Welsh *llan,* a common place-name associated with a church, and *Tegan* that often mutates to *degan,* as in 'Llandegan', and is probably the name of a Welsh saint.

the M53 motorway before passing beneath it.

Further on, the track goes under a railway line and then continues uneventfully to the village of Landican Ⓐ.

When the lane reaches a road, on the edge of Landican, turn left. Just before the first building on the left,

PUBLIC TRANSPORT Bus services to Storeton
REFRESHMENTS None on route
PUBLIC TOILETS None on route
ORDNANCE SURVEY MAPS Explorer 266 (Wirral & Chester), Landranger 108 (Liverpool)

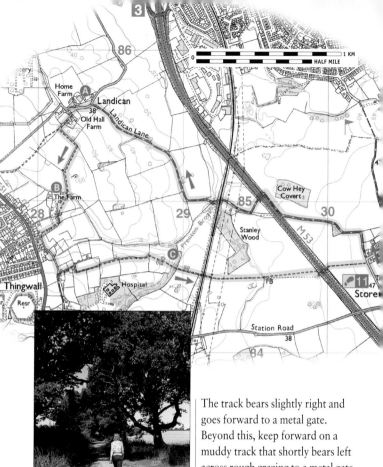

Along Storeton lanes

The track bears slightly right and goes forward to a metal gate. Beyond this, keep forward on a muddy track that shortly bears left across rough grazing to a metal gate.

Directly after the gate, turn right along a field edge (waymarked). After about ¼ mile (400m) the edge-side path reaches a step-stile in a field corner, beyond which a foot-bridge spans a narrow stream **B**.

leave the road by bearing left on to a stony track and then take the right-hand of two options, on to a footpath signposted to Thingwall.

In the ensuing field, go forward to pass in front of an isolated bungalow and keep on across the field to a wooden kissing-gate giving on to a stony track.

Cross the end of the track and go through another gate on to an enclosed path-way to a stile.

Fields near Landican

Turn right, on a stony track through a caravan storage area, and go forward past a large greenhouse. At the end of the track, turn left on to a surfaced track leading briefly to a stile giving on to a lane.

Go ahead along a narrow lane. When the lane forks, at Woodfinlow Cottage, bear left on a signposted path for Storeton. The lane begins as a broad, stony track between hedgerows, but after about 150 yds (137m) it bends right and becomes a narrow path.

Keep forward over stiles and by a clear route along field edges to enter a large field. Here, bear right to pass a small pond enclosed by trees and undergrowth. Beyond this, descend to a step-stile at a woodland edge **C**.

Cross a footbridge and go up steps. Then keep forward on a field edge path that soon passes another pond, beyond which the path continues through light under-growth.

Maintain the same direction and soon reach and cross with care a railway line. Continue on the other side on a field-edge path before crossing an open field. On the far side, cross a wooden footbridge and continue along a clear path across the ensuing pasture, aiming for a bridge over the motorway.

On the other side of the motorway, go straight across the next field, aiming for a black and white foot-path signpost in the distance. At the signpost, turn right to return to the start.   ●

12 Willaston and the Wirral Way

START Hadlow Station, Willaston

DISTANCE 4¾ miles (7.6km)

TIME 2 hours

PARKING Free car park at rear of Hadlow station

ROUTE FEATURES Old railway trackbed, some road walking, farm tracks and field paths

Apart from the need to safeguard against approaching traffic on the few road sections, this walk is a delight, passing through attractive farmland, and wandering around lanes to visit an old windmill (now a private house) and Willaston village.

🥾 Begin from the car park at the rear of the disused but well-preserved Hadlow Railway Station.

Hadlow Railway Station is the only station along the former railway line to have retained its original platform buildings, and these have been lovingly restored, along with the Waiting Room and Ticket Office.

The trackbed is flanked by mixed hedgerows and wild flowers, and leads on beneath a bridge into heavier woodland cover.

Walk to the far end of the car park and turn right through a gap on to the Wirral Way, and then turn right again to walk towards the railway station.

Walk past the station, cross the main road with care, and continue along the surfaced Wirral Way on the other side, part of the original railway trackbed.

Keep on through a narrow underpass beneath the A540, and on the other side go through a gate on the right to continue the route.

Immediately after crossing a wooden footbridge **A**, leave the trackbed by descending, right, on to a bridleway, and bear left along it. Follow this until it meets a road near a car park (on the left).

PUBLIC TRANSPORT Bus services to Willaston

REFRESHMENTS Pubs and cafés in Willaston

PUBLIC TOILETS In ticket office at station

ORDNANCE SURVEY MAPS Explorer 266 (Wirral & Chester), Landranger 117 (Chester & Wrexham)

Turn right along the road, taking care against approaching traffic in the absence of verges, and walk up to meet the A540. Turn left for 100 yds (91m), opposite the Hinderton Mount **B**, cross the road with care to a signposted footpath on the other side.

Cross a stone stile, and go up the left-hand edge of the ensuing field to two gates in quick succession at the top of the field, giving on to a quiet country lane. Turn right.

Continue along the road for about 500 yds (457m) and, when it bends sharply right, leave it on the apex by turning on to a surfaced lane **C**, going past Rose House and shortly Roselea Farm. When the road surfacing ends, keep forward on a

> **?** *This stretch of the Wirral Way forms part of the National Cycle Network, which is made up of a number of different cycle routes. What number does this route have?*

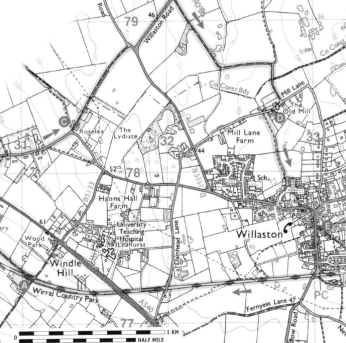

path flanked by hedgerows.

Follow the path until it meets a road and there turn right. Almost immediately turn left into Willaston Road and follow this road for about ¼ mile (400m). As it bends left, leave the main road for a signposted footpath on the right, for Willaston.

The path changes direction a couple of times but continues to head for Willaston. Eventually it reaches Mill Lane, opposite a row of cottages. Turn right and go past the Old Mill **D**.

Continue along the lane for about 150 yds (137m) and then leave it,

over a step-stile on the left at another footpath signposted for Willaston. Go forward along the left-hand field edge to another step-stile giving on to a narrow, enclosed path leading to a wooden kissing-gate. This leads into a school playing-field.

Keep along the left-hand edge of the field and, at the far side, continue on to a waymarked path. The path leads between houses on to the lawned edge of a small estate. Cross diagonally left to a broad lane leading past the church to a footpath giving on to the centre of Willaston village.

Turn left to the junction with Hadlow Road and there turn right, passing the Old Hall **E** and 16th-century Ash Tree Farm, a timber-framed, wattle-and-daub building on the left. Keep on down the road to reach the entrance to the station car park.   ●

Willaston

START Hadlow Station, Willaston
DISTANCE 4 miles (6.4km)
TIME 2 hours
PARKING Free car park at rear of Hadlow station
ROUTE FEATURES Old railway trackbed, some road walking, farm tracks and field paths

The great pleasure of this walk comes from wandering agreeably across farmland well-populated with birds, butterflies, dragonflies and the occasional small furry animal.

Leave the Hadlow station car park at the far end by turning through a gap on to the Wirral Way. Go left for about 30 yds (27m) to a stile on the right giving into a small farm field. Cross this, keeping to the right-hand edge, to a step-stile on to a farm access.

Cross into the next field. Walk down its right edge until another stile gives on to New Hey Lane, surfaced.

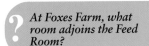

? *At Foxes Farm, what room adjoins the Feed Room?*

Turn right along the lane for about 140 yds (128m) and then leave it at a signposted path on the left. Cross a stile and go down the right-hand edge of a large open pasture.

Keep on to a step-stile in a field corner and then go straight across the next field, aiming to the left of two bungalows ahead **A**. Cross a tarmacked access and keep forward soon to pass another large house to reach a stile.

Over the stile keep on alongside a high brick wall and go down to another step-stile in the right-hand

PUBLIC TRANSPORT Bus services to Willaston
REFRESHMENTS Pubs and cafés in Willaston; café at Foxes Farm
PUBLIC TOILETS In ticket office at station
ORDNANCE SURVEY MAPS Explorer 266 (Wirral & Chester), Landranger 117 (Chester & Wrexham)

field corner.
Beyond this, maintain the same direction across an open field, aiming for a metal gate and stile on the far side.

Climb the stile and turn left along the ensuing field boundary to another stile in a corner.

Across this stile, turn immediately right to follow the field edge and divert a little to pass a pond before continuing to meet the A540 road at a narrow step-stile through a substantial hedgerow.

B Turn left to follow the A-road for about 500 yds (457m) until almost opposite the turning to Ness Gardens. Go left here through a metal kissing-gate and up the right-hand edge of successive fields until the right-hand hedgerow ends at a hedge gap giving on a large open field.

Go forward across the field to a signpost on the opposite side (this field is sometimes cropped over, but you are entitled to follow the course of the right-of-way). On the other side, turn right for 100 yds (91m), as far as a broad track on the left.

Turn left towards Foxes Farm **C**, which is entered at a metal gate. A waymarked route leads through the farmyard.

Back on the main route, follow a concrete road on to Hallwood Farm. Immediately after the farm, go through a metal gate and on to a narrow, enclosed footpath running alongside the driveway. This leads to a narrow sleeper bridge and step-stile in a hedgerow, over which the path continues up the right-hand edge of the next field

Foxes Farm is now a riding-school, but walkers are welcome and, by turning right past the stables, an isolated building, a café can be reached (open Tue–Sun 10.15–16.30).

to a field corner stile giving on to a narrow, surfaced lane.

Turn left along the lane. Eventually the surfacing ends and the continuing track is stony. It leads to a road junction. Here, turn left (signposted for Willaston). Follow the road, which gradually starts to climb to cross the course of the Wirral Way.

Continue for another 100 yds (91m) and then turn sharp left on to a signposted cycleway leading back to join the Wirral Way.

On reaching the Wirral Way, turn right and follow this unerringly back to the start.

On the Wirral Way, Willaston

14 *Raven Meols Hills*

START Victoria Road, Formby

DISTANCE 3½ miles (5.6km)

TIME 2 hours

PARKING National Trust car park at end of Victoria Road

ROUTE FEATURES Roads, woodland paths, tracks, sand-dunes and beach

Making the most of the fine beach and dune walking, this route explores a nature reserve popular with the rare natterjack toad and visits a small wildlife area populated with ducks and seabirds. Note: at certain times of year, jellyfish and weaver fish become stranded on the beach or in the shallows and are capable of stinging anyone who stands on them bare-footed. Always ensure that children on the beach wear shoes or sandals.

From the car park walk through the dunes towards the beach and turn left along it.

Continue along the beach for about 1 mile (1.6km) to a beacon with a sign-post pointing to 'Car Park: Information'. Go past this and another one to reach a third beacon.

On reaching the third beacon Ⓐ,

Many **waders, gulls and migrant birds** feed along the shoreline here. The semi-fossilised hoofprints of the **auroch**, a huge, now extinct, beast that grazed the saltmarshes during Neolithic times, are sometimes exposed in the inter-tidal sediments.

leave the beach by climbing through the dunes on to an enclosed sandy path through an area much-favoured by the natterjack toad, which is instantly recognisable by a bright yellow stripe along its back.

Stick to the sandy path, which eventually reaches Lifeboat Road car park. Follow the car park access, which

PUBLIC TRANSPORT Rail and bus services to Freshfield (the walk can start from the station), then NT Beach bus service from station

REFRESHMENTS Pubs and cafés in Formby; ice-cream vendors visit the car park

PUBLIC TOILETS Within woodland, adjoining main access

ORDNANCE SURVEY MAPS Explorer 285 (Southport & Chorley, Wigan, Formby), Landranger 108 (Liverpool)

starts left then swings round to the right and soon joins surfaced Lifeboat Road. Turn left and continue past the entrance to Formby Point Caravan Park.

About 50 yds (46m) after the caravan park, leave the road by turning left at a permissive bridle-path (signposted) through trees. A broad path now runs through light woodland. As it emerges from the woodland, it meets a

? *What is the name of the sea on the right?*

cross-path (steps on the right here, ignore these). Keep forward across open heathland.

Always keep going forward, and this eventually leads to a reedy pond **B**, a small wildlife area with ducks, coots and

moorhens in abundance. Cross the bridge over the pond and turn right along a boardwalk.

Beyond the end of the pond, keep going forward, ignoring side paths, and soon climb a short flight of steps. At the top, bear left along an enclosed sandy path that soon descends gently through woodland to the rear of a modern housing estate.

The continuing path becomes a broad track and leads finally out of the woodland to the edge of a surfaced road. Here turn left into Larkhill Lane.

Within the last 200 years many areas within the Formby dunes were levelled by farmers growing **asparagus**. In the 1930s, Formby asparagus was a popular delicacy served to passengers on luxury liners leaving from Liverpool. Then there were more than 200 acres (81 ha) of asparagus fields along this stretch of coast. Now there are no more than five.

Walk along Larkhill Lane as far as Blundell Avenue, and then turn left. The road leads through open pine woodland, and passes Sandfield Farm **C**. About 50 yds (46m) after the farm entrance, as the main road swings left, leave it and take the right-hand of two paths, a surfaced pathway through coastal woodland with open fields on the right formerly used for growing asparagus.

Continue with the path as it heads for Nicotine Wood, through which it wanders agreeably. Always keep following the most pronounced path, which eventually meets up with the sign-posted 'Woodland Path' **D**. Ignore this and keep left through sand-dunes soon to emerge at the Victoria Road car park at the starting point of the walk. ●

Beach at Raven Meols Hills

Frodsham Edge and Overton Hill

With expansive views across the Mersey Estuary and beyond, this fine walk wanders the wooded sandstone escarpment above Frodsham and visits the site of an Iron Age hillfort.

START Beacon Hill, Frodsham

DISTANCE 3¼ miles (5.2km)

TIME 1½–2 hours

PARKING Beacon Hill car park

ROUTE FEATURES Woodland paths, farm tracks and fields, rocky outcrops

15

Leave the Beacon Hill car park and turn left down the road for about 200 yds (183m) and then turn left on to a driveway (signposted to Frodsham and Bellemonte) to Overhill Cottage.

Walk past the cottage and go forward on a grassy path leading to a gate. Beyond the gate walk up to a hotel driveway, go across it and on to a waymarked path on the other side, alongside a fence. The path descends in stages to meet a road Ⓐ.

At the road, turn right and walk down to the Belle Monte pub. Turn left here and, just beyond the pub car park, turn right on to a descending path into woodland. Almost immediately leave this path by bearing left on to a path along the top edge of the woodland (signposted: Mersey View via Ladies Walk).

When the path forks, keep left on the higher path and continue to another waymark at which the continuing path forks again. Climb left here, on a twisting path that leads up to a war memorial, just beyond which a topograph Ⓑ

PUBLIC TRANSPORT Bus and rail services to Frodsham

REFRESHMENTS In Frodsham and pub on route

PUBLIC TOILETS None on route

ORDNANCE SURVEY MAPS Explorer 267 (Northwich & Delamere Forest, Winsford), Landranger 117 (Chester & Wrexham)

points out various places that can be seen.

Go past the topograph and on to a sandy path through gorse, oak, rowan and birch. When the path forks, bear right, descending.

The continuing route is clearly marked by yellow waymarks as the path wanders easily along below the sandstone escarpment of Frodsham Edge, shaded by woodland.

Just after a recess on the left **C**, the path climbs to run alongside a farm field. Alongside this farm field take care to guard against stumbling over the remains of fence stanchions protruding from the path, particularly as they are difficult to spot.

The path eventually reaches a path junction. Here turn right, descending towards

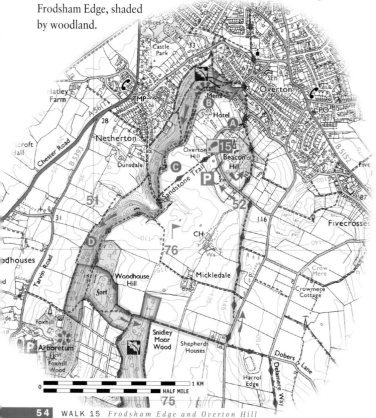

Woodhouse Hill. (Anyone wanting to shorten the walk can simply turn left here and follow a clear path, signposted to Beacon Hill, to meet the road about 100 yds (91m) north of the Beacon Hill car park.)

 Many of the waymarks are marked with a letter 'S', signifying that this is part of the **Sandstone Trail**, a 30-mile (48km) walk linking Beacon Hill with the northern edge of the Shropshire Way at Grindley Brook.

alongside the boundary wall of an Iron Age hillfort on Woodhouse Hill, along which the route is clearly waymarked.

The path continues to cling to the top edge of the woodland but soon goes down a flight of steps known as the Baker's Dozen.

? *How many are there in a baker's dozen?*

At the bottom of the Baker's Dozen, more steps (Jacob's Ladder) await, below which, near a sandstone cliff, the track forks. Branch left on to a broad sandy path.

The continuing path leads to a rocky dead end, with the path climbing easily up a small rock outcrop **D**. Above this, go forward at the top edge of woodland alongside a golf course.

Just after a bench, at a viewpoint, the path forks again. Bear left, climbing into more woodland. Keep forward and soon walk

The way continues along a woodland boundary. At the edge of Snidley Moor Wood the path forks, with the Sandstone Trail here going right. Leave the Trail now and go left into Snidley Moor Wood (a Woodland Trust property).

The war memorial at Frodsham Edge

A view of Helsby Hill from Overton Hill

On the far side of the wood the path forks once more. Keep ahead, on the left branch, to walk along a hedgerowed path leading to a gate. Beyond this, go forward along a broad farm access that leads out to a road.

Turn left for about 200 yds (183m) to a waymarked stile and path on the left.

Over the stile, bear half-right across the middle of a field aiming for radio masts on Beacon Hill. Walk across the field to two stiles, one either side of a farm access. After the second stile, keep forward on an enclosed path.

When the path gives into an open field, go forward along the left-hand field edge to a gap in a field corner giving on to a road. Turn left and follow the road back to the Beacon Hill car park. ●

Hale and the Mersey

START Hale
DISTANCE 5 miles (8km)
TIME 2 hours
PARKING Limited roadside parking adjacent to St Mary's Church (please park considerately)
ROUTE FEATURES Road walking, quiet lanes, farm paths

16

Lying directly beneath the flight path for Liverpool Airport, this walk is frequently overshadowed by aircraft coming in to land or taking off. Such road walking as there is, is agreeable, and soon leads to a splendid foreshore walk with expansive views over the Mersey Estuary.

From the church, go towards the village centre, along Church Road, following this round to the Childe of Hale pub. At the nearby road junction, keep forward into High Street.

Follow the main road as it bends left (signed Trans-Pennine Trail) into Hale Road Ⓐ. Continue along Hale Road for about ½ mile (800m) and then turn left into Baileys Lane.

? *Along Hale Road, Brook Farm is passed. How old is this farm?*

In St Mary's churchyard is the grave of **John Middleton** (1578–1623), a renowned wrestler, known as the **'Childe of Hale'**, who stood 9ft 3in (2.8m) tall. He is also commemorated outside the churchyard in the form of a huge wooden carving representing the man and events significant to the village.

Go down Baileys Lane to a T-junction, and there turn left. A short way on, when the road forks at the entrance to Mersey Way Conservation Area, branch left on to a track leading to a metal gate, giving on to a path through scrub descending to the foreshore.

PUBLIC TRANSPORT Bus services to Hale
REFRESHMENTS Pubs and village shop in Hale
PUBLIC TOILETS None on route
ORDNANCE SURVEY MAPS Explorer 275 (Liverpool, St Helens, Widnes & Runcorn), Landranger 108 (Liverpool)

B Just before reaching the foreshore, turn left on to a gently rising path that runs along an embankment above the salt-marshes.

The path then continues easily, eventually reaching a flight of wooden steps going down to an in-flowing stream. Continue up steps on the other side and resume following the path, which now runs along the edge of a large arable pasture.

The continuing path occasionally dips in and out of light woodland, always parallel with the foreshore. Gradually the path descends as it

> The **Mersey Estuary** is a Site of Special Scientific Interest, one of Britain's top sites for birds. Thousands of birds visit here, flying from as far away as Greenland, Siberia, Scandinavia and Iceland to spend the winter. The mud is teeming with worms and shellfish, which are highly nutritious. You can see shelduck, oystercatcher, mallard, heron, redshank, dunlin, sandpiper, curlew and, occasionally in winter, teal. The Mersey is at its widest near the lighthouse, giving spectacular changing views across to Frodsham and Helsby, and the Clwydian Hills.

St Mary's Church, Hale

The memorial to the 'Childe of Hale'

leading into a narrow surfaced lane.

At the end of the lane (Within Way), turn left into Church Road to return to the starting point at the village church. ●

For centuries the ford at Within Way was the only reasonably safe crossing place of the **River Mersey** for people with animals. The dangers encountered can only be imagined. The area to the east of Hale Ford and towards what is now known as Widnes was in those ancient times extensive naturally draining marshland stretching several miles inland, criss-crossed with deep gullies. Graves in Hale churchyard testify that lives were regularly lost in crossing the Mersey before bridges were built.

approaches Hale lighthouse, first built in 1836, but now closed, where a lane leads off, left, towards Hale village (ignore this).

Cross to a gate at the rear of the lighthouse, and continue on a pleasant path, again sandwiched between arable land and the salt-marshes. This eventually reaches Within Way, at a wooden gate.

Turn left, here, leaving the fore-shore, and walk towards the village of Hale. Beyond another gate, the path becomes a broader track

17 *Thurstaston and Caldy*

START Thurstaston Visitor Centre

DISTANCE 6½ miles (10.5km)

TIME 3 hours

PARKING Adjoining visitor centre

ROUTE FEATURES Old trackbed, field paths and woodland tracks

This, the longest walk in this book, is best reserved for a sunny day, for then the woodland and fields are alive with bird-song and the pastures bright with flowers. Much of Thurstaston Common is a blaze of purple and gold with heather and gorse in August and September.

Start from the car park close to the visitor centre at Thurstaston by walking across the car park to the trackbed of the former station. Turn left on to a rising path that then continues past a campsite.

Just after the end of the campsite, turn left on a narrow path (way-marked in red, yellow and blue) that leads up to the old railway trackbed. It is now part of the elongated Wirral Country Park.

Follow the trackbed for about ½ mile (800m), as far as a sign-posted footpath on the left (it is waymarked blue and yellow) **A**. Here go down steps and

From Victorian times a popular railway linked Hooton, on the main Chester to Birkenhead line, to West Kirby. Steam trains brought townspeople out to Parkgate and the seaside on cheap day excursions and took back coal from Neston colliery, potatoes and milk. But by 1962 the line was closed. The Dee Estuary had silted up, the colliery was shut and the car had replaced the train. In 1973 the old line was opened as **Wirral Country Park**, one of the first country parks in Britain.

PUBLIC TRANSPORT Bus services to Thurstaston

REFRESHMENTS Shop and café at start; pub at Thurstaston

PUBLIC TOILETS At start; in visitor centre

ORDNANCE SURVEY MAPS Explorer 266 (Wirral & Chester), Landranger 108 (Liverpool)

Cemy

B 5140

37

Royden Park
(Country Park)

C
Hill Bark

P

Stapledon
Wood

86

D

FB

Sch

28
MP

Thurstaston Common

Irby Hill

63

85

B 5140

Benty
Farm

23

CH

24

Thurstaston
Hill

Sch

25

P

Thurstaston

MP
B

Rec

Dawpool
Farm

84

23

Station Road

Thurstaston
Hall

52

Telegraph R

Caravan
Park

The
Dungeon

Shore Cottage

28

P

17

V
PC

80

40

35

30

25

Waterfall

83

Wirral Way

Wirral
Country
Park

22

A

Old

Piper

0   1 KM

HALF MILE

'The Guardian of the Visitor Centre', Thurstaston

Thurstaston, crossing a stile that gives on to an enclosed path.

Keep following the path over stiles and through a kissing-gate, with a good view out across the Dee Estuary and ahead to the sandstone steeple of Thurstaston parish church.

forward along a constructed pathway that eventually leads into woodland surrounding a narrow, mossy ravine known as the Dungeon.

Immediately on entering the woodland, go left into a Conservation Area, climbing steps.

At the top of the steps, turn right and follow a gently rising path above the ravine, which often has an attractive waterfall at its head. Above this, cross a wooden footbridge, and beyond continue along the woodland boundary.

The continuing path is in parts paved with concrete slabs. Elsewhere old railway sleepers have been put to good use, though these can be slippery when wet. At the far end of the wood, turn left on a path signposted for

Eventually the path descends to a concrete step-stile that gives on to a earthen track leading into the edge of Thurstaston village.

Keep forward, now on a broad stony track to meet a road. Continue forward past St Bartholomew's Church.

After the church, take the next turning on the right and walk up to join the A540 **B**.

At a road junction, turn left into Telegraph Road. Cross the road

> **St Bartholomew's Church** was redeveloped in Victorian times (1885), and is, in the author's opinion, one of few attractive churches to date from this period. In the churchyard, a battlemented tower dates from a Georgian (1824) rebuilding.

with care and go past the Cottage Loaf pub. About 100 yds (91m) further on, bear right into the National Trust Thurstaston Common Nature Reserve on a footpath signposted to Royden Park.

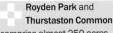

Royden Park and **Thurstaston Common** comprise almost 250 acres (100 ha) of semi-natural and planted woodland, heathland and open parkland.

The continuing path becomes a broad sandy track that eventually meets the end of a surfaced lane. Go forward through the right-hand of two gates to enter light woodland.

Follow the main path, going forward, soon passing through bracken before emerging on to a broad track. Go left to pass Benty Farm.

Stay on the track, pass through a gate and kissing-gate, beyond which, when the track forks, bear left. Keep following the track as far as the end of a sandstone wall. Go across the end of the wall on to another broad track, this time giving into a large field.

Keep to the left-hand edge of the field, now part of Royden Park Country Park **C**.

Continue to a wooden barrier and then cross the next field. Walk out to a car park access. Turn left to a road junction, and there turn right. Almost immediately go left on a path signposted to Montgomery Hill and Frankby Mere.

Go forward through a metal barrier and keep on along the track until it emerges at another road.

Turn right for 100 yds (91m) and then go left on a path for Newton (ignore the path for Grange). Initially a wide, stony track, the route goes past the entrance to Royden Manor and becomes a surfaced lane for a short while before becoming a rough track once more.

The track bends right and left, running alongside a sandstone wall, and leads down to a gate and sandstone step-stile, beyond which it continues down the edge of an arable field.

Follow the field edge as far as a step-stile on the right. Over this, cross a narrow footbridge, and follow an equally and seasonally overgrown narrow path between a high fence and an established hedgerow. Eventually the path

As the walk heads into Thurstaston village, one of the farm buildings has an interesting weather-vane. What two animals does it depict?

passes out between houses on to an estate road (Grange Cross Lane).

Turn left to a T-junction **D** and there turn right. Cross the road with care and walk gently uphill. Go past Footpath 48 and continue as far as Kings Drive North, and here turn left.

When the road ends, go forward into woodland keeping left at first, but when the track forks a short way on, at a waymark sign, bear right along a bridleway.

The bridleway goes through mixed woodland, and eventually emerges at the end of a surfaced lane (Kings Drive), flanked by Lottery-winners' dream houses. At the end of Kings Drive, turn left and follow the road as it winds down to meet the B5140 near Caldy centre, at a T-junction.

Cross the road, towards a bench and bus-stop opposite, and go down sandstone steps to gain a descending path to the right of the Croft. Continue down the path, once more in woodland.

The path descends to meet another road. Turn right, go across the end of Barton Hey Drive, and, opposite the entrance to Wirral Country Park car park, turn left just before the railway bridge abutments on to a gently rising path (waymarked) to rejoin the old railway trackbed.

Now simply follow the trackbed, using the right-hand of two paths (the other is for horses and cyclists), and this leads unerringly back to the disused Thurstaston station at the start of the walk. ●

St Bartholomew's Church, Thurstaston

Parkgate

18

START Parkgate
DISTANCE 5½ miles (8.9km)
TIME 2½ hours
PARKING Off Mostyn Square and School Lane
ROUTE FEATURES Seafront paths, estate road, field paths and graded trackway

With virtually no height gain, this delightfully easy walk saunters along the seafront at Parkgate, as holidaymakers have done for hundreds of years, and then makes good use of a former railway line flanked by a wide variety of wild flowers in season.

🖊 Begin from the car park off Mostyn Square and walk out to the foreshore, turning left along the Parade. Go past Mostyn House School, beyond which the main road bears left.

Continue along the seafront, and, after the end of the road, take to a raised path 🅐 along the seawall at the edge of the marshes. This leads between houses to a surfaced road.

Turn right and follow the road to a narrow, enclosed path, maintaining the same direction and leading shortly into Manorial Road South.

🏁 **Parkgate** looks like a Victorian seaside resort, a long seafront of terraced houses, shops, hotels and the Parade, which is a ½-mile- (800-m) long promenade. More than fifty years ago, the sea abandoned Parkgate, and what was once golden sand became grassy marshes.

The rapid silting of the River Dee was more than partially to blame for Parkgate's decline, but so, too, was the improvement of roads through North Wales and Holyhead, which afforded a shorter and less hazardous route to Ireland.

By the end of the Second World War, the encroaching marshes finally reached the seawall. But until then, Parkgate was still a popular sea-bathing resort.

PUBLIC TRANSPORT Bus services to Parkgate (Mostyn Square)
REFRESHMENTS Pubs, cafés and restaurants at Parkgate
PUBLIC TOILETS Adjoining car park
ORDNANCE SURVEY MAPS Explorer 266 (Wirral & Chester), Landranger 117 (Chester & Wrexham)

0   1 KM
HALF MILE

? *How old would you have to be to attend Mostyn House School?*

Keep on down this road until it bends sharply left and here leave it for a signposted footpath on the right ('Old quay ½ mile'), leading down to the foreshore.

On reaching the foreshore, turn left on to a narrow path. This leads to a low step-stile and continues beyond to reach the remains of the Old Quay **B**, there crossing an in-flowing stream by a narrow wooden footbridge.

Immediately over the bridge, go forward on a grassy path, aiming for the left-hand of three tall trees among hedgerows in the middle distance. As the tree is reached, turn left on a clear path. This leads

The **Old Quay** is all that remains of the 16th-century port that flourished here, now completely landlocked. In the mid-16th century the water here was deep, providing a safe anchorage, but there were problems associated with its development, and gradually the Old Quay fell into disrepair.

to a wooden sleeper bridge spanning a stream. Occasionally the bridge is flooded but is rarely impassable.

Cross, head along an obvious but boggy path, aiming for a powerline pole in mid-field. Keep on in the same direction to reach a hedge-enclosed path. A short way along this, turn right through a metal kissing-gate (yellow waymark) and cross the ensuing field to the left-hand of three hedge gaps ahead.

Keep to the left-hand margin of the next field and follow a narrow path up to a gate giving on to the Wirral Way, a broad, graded and level path **C**. Turn left.

Now follow the Wirral Way until it emerges at a gate on to a surfaced lane. Go forward to the main road and turn right for about 30 yds (27m). Turn left into the Ropewalk, and, immediately before the first house on the right, leave the road for a cobbled and waymarked path through trees passing to the rear of the house, and soon rejoining the Wirral Way.

Stay on the Wirral Way as it crosses first Brooklands Road Bridge **D** and then goes beneath Blackwood Hall Bridge. Keep going to reach a bridge with three rectangular arches. Here, leave the Wirral Way by turning right up broad steps to reach a road. Turn left to cross the bridge and follow the road down to its end, overlooking the marshes.

A short flight of steps leads left on to another raised path along the seawall, for the most part with a golf course on the left. This eventually leads to a gate on the left giving into an elongated car park on the site of the Old Baths **E**.

Go through the car park and out along its access to meet the main road near the Boat House pub.

Keep forward along the Parade as far as the Marsh Cat Restaurant, and there turn left to return to the car park in School Lane. ●

The wide open marshes of the **Dee Estuary** look barren but are a safe haven for thousands of migrant and resident shore birds.

● Wildfowl ● old railway trackbed ● botanic gardens with rare plants

19 *Neston*

START Ness Botanic Gardens

DISTANCE 5¾ miles (9.3km)

TIME 2½ hours

PARKING Ness Gardens (assuming you will visit the gardens)

ROUTE FEATURES Coastal paths, farm fields, track-bed, country lanes

Liverpool cotton-broker Arthur Bulley built his house on a sandstone outcrop above the River Dee and, in so doing, laid the foundations of Ness Gardens. His great desire was to bring new plant species into Britain, especially those from the Alps and Himalayas. The result is a delight – and likely to add a few hours to your day.

Begin from the car park at Ness Botanic Gardens and turn right along the main road. At the next junction, turn right into Denhall Lane and follow this down to the foreshore.

At the foreshore, turn right again, along a narrow, surfaced lane, which is a signposted footpath parallel with the foreshore. The lane surfacing eventually ends, but a track continues forward, still along the foreshore, and becomes a narrow path that runs on to become a broad track along the edge of a housing estate at Nessholt.

The continuing lane passes the Harp Inn **A**. On reaching the last of the houses at Little Neston, keep forward on a wide track beyond a metal gate. Gradually, the route degenerates to

Ahead, beyond the Dee Estuary, rise the **Clwydian Hills** of North Wales. Their highest point is Moel Famau.

PUBLIC TRANSPORT Bus services to Ness Gardens entrance

REFRESHMENTS In Ness Gardens and the Harp Inn

PUBLIC TOILETS Ness Gardens

ORDNANCE SURVEY MAPS Explorer 266 (Wirral & Chester), Landranger 117 (Chester & Wrexham)

? *The foreshore here is the Dee Wildfowl Reserve, and has been maintained since 1964 by an organisation. What is its name?*

a narrow path between reedbeds and an established hawthorn hedgerow on the right.

The path leads to a sandstone step-stile on the edge of the site of the Old Quay **B** (see Walk 18 Parkgate). Over the stile, turn right on an obvious path along the edge of scrubland, which then goes forward alongside a hawthorn hedge. This leads to a sleeper bridge across a stream (sometimes flooded but rarely impassable),

beyond which the path heads for an overhead powerline pole in mid-field.

Continue across the field in the same direction to a path enclosed by high hedgerows. Turn into this, but after only a few strides leave the path at a metal kissing-gate on the right, and head to the left-hand of three hedge gaps ahead (the one nearest another powerline pole concealed in a hedgerow).

Go up the left-hand edge of the ensuing field to a gate in the top left corner **C**. Here, through a kissing-gate, turn right on to the Wirral Way, which follows a former railway trackbed.

Azaleas in Ness Botanic Gardens

The way soon reaches a small car park. Go forward beneath a nearby railway bridge, and then walk along the ensuing road, at the edge of a small housing estate.

At the far end of Station Road, go on to meet a main road (Bushell Road). Cross with care to rejoin the Wirral

Way opposite, walking once more along the former railway trackbed.

The trackbed goes forward under a high single-arched bridge and further on passes beneath a low arched bridge, beyond which it enters the Wirral Country Park.

Still following the trackbed, keep going as far as a wooden bridge **D**, and here leave the trackbed by descending on the right track. Over a stile, turn right along a wide track and, when this narrows down to a path between hedgerows, keep forward on to the path.

Stay with the path until it bends sharply right, go left through a metal kissing-gate and then forward along the right-hand edge of a large field on a signposted footpath. The field edge is a guide to a step-stile giving on to a narrow enclosed path that leads to another metal kissing-gate.

Through the gate, turn left on to a rough lane (Woodfall Lane). Follow it round to meet a surfaced lane (Mill Lane) opposite Hilltop Farm. In places Mill Lane is single track with passing-places. Keep children (and animals) under close control against approaching traffic.

Go along the lane as far as a speed restriction sign, and there turn sharply left into Flashes Lane. After the lane surfacing ends, go forward to a signed footpath about 40 yds (37m) further on. Turn right, now a narrow path between hedgerows.

When the path comes out to meet a lane at Orchard House, turn right and walk to the main road. Turn left to return to Ness Gardens. ●

An archway in Ness Botanic Gardens

20 *Blundellsands and Hightown*

START Seafront, Blundellsands (end of Hall Road)
DISTANCE 6 miles (9.7km)
TIME 2½ hours
PARKING Seafront car park
ROUTE FEATURES Road walking, farm tracks, coastal sand-dunes and paths

Entirely level, this easy walk loops around the coastal countryside before returning along the edge of Liverpool Bay. The road walking requires children (and animals) to be kept under close control and leads into Hightown, where it meets up with the Sefton Coastal Footpath.

Start from the large seafront car park adjacent to the coastguard station at the western end of Hall Road. Leave the car park along its access and turn left into Hall Road West.

Follow the road past the entrance to West Lancashire Golf Club and go forward at Hall Road railway station.

At the far end of Hall Road, where it bends sharply right, leave it, going forward on to a signposted bridleway to Little Crosby. At first the path is enclosed by hedgerows, but then breaks free and continues, heading for the steeple of Little Crosby church, as a broad track across arable fields.

As the continuing track ends Ⓐ, at the edge of Little Crosby, turn right for about 150 yds (137m) to visit

The cross on the right is an **ancient preaching cross**; that on the left is a crucifix and a memorial to Squire Francis Nicholas Blundell, who lived at Crosby Hall.

PUBLIC TRANSPORT Rail and bus services to Hall Road or Hightown (alternative start)
REFRESHMENTS Hotel and corner shop in Hightown; possibly ice-cream van at start
PUBLIC TOILETS At start
ORDNANCE SURVEY MAPS Explorer 285 (Southport & Chorley, Wigan, Formby), Landranger 108 (Liverpool)

The seashore at Blundellsands

Hamgate Farm

D

PO

Hightown

Sports Ground

Sandy Ln

C

Dunes

03

Gorsey Lane

Moss Farm

Wood Farm

B

Flea Moss Wood

Moss Lane

B5193

Woodham Knoll

30

31

32

Dunes

Sniggery Farm

02

Hill Farm

A

Little Crosby

Dunes

Sniggery Wood

Ackers Lane

Dibb Lane

Little Cro

Far Moss Pool

Sefton Coastal Footpath

Playing Field

01

Sniggery Wood

Sch

CG Sta

CH

Hall Road Station

P 20

Scho

0   1 KM
HALF MILE

two crosses almost opposite one another.

 How old was Squire Blundell when he died?

Go back towards Little Crosby, turning right at the road bend and walking towards St Mary's Catholic Church.

On reaching the church, go left into Moss Lane (signposted to Hightown). Once the pavement ends, take great care along this busy road and keep children and animals under close control.

When Moss Lane turns sharply to the right, leave it by turning left into Gorsey Lane **B** and walking along the edge of Flea Moss Wood.

Continue to follow the road until reaching Moss Farm, and there leave it by turning right on to a signposted path for Sandy Lane. This leads across farm fields towards the village of Hightown. After about 250 yds (229m) the track makes a shallow S-bend, and here the right of way leaves the main track, turning right, into reedbeds. Follow the narrow path **C** (low, yellow waymark on the right) until it runs out beside a cottage to a T-junction.

Turn right along a broad path and follow it left, continuing past two sports grounds on to a surfaced lane that leads into the edge of Hightown. Go across the end of Elmcroft Lane and continue to pass a low, white church on the left.

Take the next turning left (Alt Road), to Hightown Station. Cross the line by the footbridge and keep forward on the other side, past the

The River Alt at Hightown

Hightown Hotel, to a road junction.

Turn right, passing the post office, and shortly go left. Walk up to a roundabout with a war memorial. Cross the end of Thornbeck Avenue and go forward into Lower Alt Road.

At the end of the road, go past a yacht club compound to meet the Sefton Coastal Path. Turn left here **D** (signposted Hall Road 2 miles), passing Alt Centre, beyond which a signposted footpath leads on, parallel with the River Alt for a short distance.

The preaching cross at Little Crosby

Soon the path moves away from the river, through reedbeds, with the continuing route waymarked by white-topped posts. This meanders through sand-dunes for some distance before reaching a small parking area.

Keep forward, staying along the

> A pair of binoculars would be useful along this section of the walk as the coast is favoured by a many species of **wading and seabirds**. The channel further out is used by ocean-going passenger and freight-carrying **ships**.

Sefton Coastal Path, which is now less sandy and more grassy underfoot. The path continues to be waymarked and leads eventually to a long, level stretch with the sea close by on the right.

The continuing route is a broad, grassy and stony track that eventually becomes a service track leading directly back to the car park at the coastguard station. ●

Further Information

Walking Safety

Although the reasonably gentle countryside that is the subject of this book offers no real dangers to walkers at any time of the year, it is still advisable to take sensible precautions and follow certain well-tried guidelines.

Always take with you both warm and waterproof clothing and sufficient food and drink. Wear suitable footwear, i.e. strong walking boots or shoes that give a good grip over stony ground, on slippery slopes and in muddy conditions. Try to obtain a local weather forecast and bear it in mind before you start. Do not be afraid to abandon your proposed route and return to your starting point in the event of a sudden and unexpected deterioration in the weather.

All the walks described in this book will be safe to do, given due care and respect, even during the winter. Indeed, a crisp, fine winter day often provides perfect walking conditions, with firm ground underfoot and a clarity unique to this time of the year.

The most difficult hazard likely to be encountered is mud, especially

The seafront at Parkgate

when walking along woodland and field paths, farm tracks and bridleways – the latter in particular can often get churned up by cyclists and horses. In summer, an additional difficulty may be narrow and overgrown paths, particularly along the edges of cultivated fields. Neither should constitute a major problem provided that the appropriate footwear is worn.

Sand-dunes at Formby

Follow the Country Code

- Enjoy the countryside and respect its life and work
- Guard against all risk of fire
- Take your litter home
- Fasten all gates
- Help to keep all water clean
- Keep your dogs under control
- Protect wildlife, plants and trees
- Keep to public paths across farmland
- Take special care on country roads
- Leave livestock, crops and machinery alone
- Make no unnecessary noise
- Use gates and stiles to cross fences, hedges and walls

(The Countryside Agency)

Useful Organisations

Council for the Protection of Rural England
Warwick House, 25 Buckingham Palace Road, London SW1W 0PP.
Tel. 020 7976 6433

Countryside Agency
John Dower House, Crescent Place, Cheltenham, Gloucestershire GL50 3RA.
Tel. 01242 521381

English Heritage
23 Savile Row, London W1X 1AB.
Tel. 0171 973 3250
www.english-heritage.org.uk

English Nature
Northminster House,
Peterborough, Cambs. PE1 1UA.
Tel. 01733 455100
E-mail: enquiries@english-nature.org.uk
www.english-nature.org.uk

National Trust
Membership and general enquiries:
PO Box 39, Bromley,
Kent BR1 3XL.
Tel. 0870 458 4000
Email:enquires@thenationaltrust.org.uk
Regional office:
The Hollens, Grasmere, Ambleside,
Cumbria LA22 9QZ
Tel. 0870 609 5391

Ordnance Survey
Romsey Road, Maybush,
Southampton SO16 4GU.
Tel. 08456 05 05 05 (Lo-call)

Public transport information
Bus services:
Tel. 0151 471 7384 (Mon–Fri 08.30-17.30)
Cheshire Bus Tel. 01244 602666
Halton Transport Tel. 0151 423 3333
Arriva Transport Tel. 0151 525 1733
Merseytravel (including rail travel)
Tel. 0151 236 7676

Ramblers' Association
2nd Floor, Camelford House,
87–90 Albert Embankment,
London SE1 7TW.
Tel. 020 7339 8500

Royal Society for the Protection of Birds (RSPB)
The Lodge, Sandy, Beds SG19 2DL. Tel. 01767 680551; Fax 01767 692365
www.rspb.org.uk

On the top of Thurstaston Hill

The marine lake at West Kirby

Tourist information:
North West Tourist Board
Swan House
Swan Meadow Road, Wigan Pier,
Wigan, WN3 5BB.
Tel. 01942 82122

Local tourist information centres
Birkenhead: 0151 67 6780
Liverpool 0906 680 6886 (calls
charged at 25p per minute)
Runcorn: 01928 576776
Warrington: 01925 632571
Southport: 01704 533333

Wirral Country Park
Tel. 0151 327 5145
E-mail: wcp@cheshire.gov.uk

Wirral Rangers
Tel. 0151 648 4371/3884

Youth Hostels Association
Trevelyan House,
Dimple Road, Matlock,
Derbyshire DE4 3YH
Tel. 01629 592600
Website: www.yha.org.uk

*Ordnance Survey Maps
of Merseyside and Wirral*
Explorer maps:
266 (Wirral & Chester)
267 (Northwich & Delamere
Forest, Winsford),
275 (Liverpool, St Helens, Widnes
& Runcorn)
285 (Southport & Chorley, Wigan,
Formby)

Landranger maps:
108 (Liverpool)
117 (Chester & Wrexham).

Answers to Questions

Walk 1: Ash.

Walk 2: 1771.

Walk 3: 13: 4 cannons, 7 muskets and 2 flint-lock pistols.

Walk 4: On the triangulation pillar on Helsby Hill.

Walk 5: The Empire State Building, New York.

Walk 6: Sunlight (Port Sunlight).

Walk 7: Hilbre Island – though there are quite a few islands, and they can be reached on foot, twice a day.

Walk 8: 15m.

Walk 9: Village stocks.

Walk 10: St Peter, Heswall and St Bartholomew, Thurstaston.

Walk 11: 1,000.

Walk 12: 56.

Walk 13: The Rug Room

Walk 14: The Irish Sea.

Walk 15: The Baker's Dozen is a flight of steps encountered on the route. Count the steps; there are thirteen. Medieval bakers were notorious for selling underweight loaves, an offence that could earn them a spell in the stocks. To combat this possibility, bakers would often add a thirteenth loaf to every order for twelve – hence the Baker's Dozen.

Walk 16: It was built in 1726, making it over 275 years old.

Walk 17: A horse and a dog (or is it a fox?)

Walk 18: From 4 to 18.

Walk 19: The Dee Wildfowlers and Wetlands Management Club.

Walk 20: 56 years and 12 days.